# STICK OUT LIKE A SORE THUMB

And Other
Expressions about
BODY PARTS

MATT DOEDEN

Illustrated by
AARON BLECHA

Lerner Publications Company
MINNEAPOLIS

Lerner Publications Company
A division of Lerner Publishing Group, Inc.
241 First Avenue North
Minneapolis, MN 55401 U.S.A.

Website address: www.lernerbooks.com


Library of Congress Cataloging-in-Publication Data

Doeden, Matt.
    Stick out like a sore thumb : and other
expressions about body parts / by Matt Doeden.
        p.    cm. — (It's Just an Expression)
    Includes index.
    ISBN 978–0–7613–7887–7 (lib. bdg. : alk. paper)
    1. English language—Idioms—Juvenile literature.
    2. Figures of speech—Juvenile literature.  I. Title.
PE1460.D647  2013
    428.1—dc23                              2011044560

Manufactured in the United States of America
1 – PC – 7/15/12

# TABLE of CONTENTS

# INTRODUCTION

Johan watched across the lunchroom as his friend Nick walked up to Cassie's table. It was Valentine's Day, and Nick was going to tell Cassie that he liked her in a Valentine's Day card. Nick made his card delivery and then sat back down by Johan.

"So how'd it go?" Johan asked.

"Terrible. I accidentally called Cassie by her sister's name when I handed her the card. Talk about **putting my foot in my mouth!** She totally **gave me the cold shoulder** after that. Her friends were all laughing at me, and I **stuck out like a sore thumb.**"

Johan put a hand on Nick's shoulder. "Don't worry, dude. You may have **taken it on the chin,** but at least you **had the guts** to go over there."

What are these two talking about? Chins, shoulders, guts, and a foot in somebody's mouth? Is this stuff supposed to make any sense? Yes! And it will just as soon as you get clued in to idioms. Idioms are phrases that mean something different from what you might think they mean. At times, they can seem super confusing. But once you learn what idioms mean—and where the phrases come from—they won't seem so crazy after all. Read on to find out all about idioms. Who knows? It just might keep you from putting your foot in *your* mouth someday!

# HAVE the GUTS

Coach Evans was staring at Katelyn. "The lacrosse team needs a goalie," she said. "Do you have the guts to try out?"

Hands and feet seem like important body parts to be a goaltender. But what do guts have to do with anything? Guts are gross and slimy, and they're buried deep inside you. How could they possibly help at a lacrosse tryout?

Coach Evans wasn't literally talking about guts. **Having the guts to do something just means you're willing to try something that's scary.** That might be singing a solo at a concert, trying a tough trick on your bike, or even just reading a spooky story when you're home alone.

Of course, we all know that bravery comes from your mind, not your guts. So how did this expression get started? Well, centuries ago, people weren't sure where courage came from. They guessed that it came from the stomach. So those with lots of courage were said to "have the guts" to face their fears.

Would you have the guts to face a challenge from this coach?

# PUT Your FOOT in Your MOUTH

Antoine got stuck watching a movie he hated last night when his sister beat him to the TV. Now he is complaining to his buddies on the school playground. "It was some story about a girl who falls in love with a zombie, and her parents won't let her date him. Talk about dumb!" he said.

Jackson groaned. "Oh, yeah, my sister loves that movie too. It's the stupidest thing I've ever seen. I don't know how anyone can watch that garbage!" Suddenly their classmate Erica went storming off. "That's my favorite movie ever!" she yelled back at the guys.

"Oops," Jackson said. "I didn't know she was listening. I didn't mean to make her mad. I guess I kind of put my foot in my mouth that time."

Mmm—what sounds yummier than a big old taste of your own sweaty foot? Probably just about anything. But don't worry. **This expression doesn't actually have anything to do with your feet. It means you've said something to embarrass yourself or someone else.** Maybe you talked badly about a friend who was standing nearby. Or maybe,

This kid totally dissed his classmate's favorite movie. Now he feels like he put his foot in his mouth.

like Jackson, you said something really negative about something someone else loves.

The meaning of this idiom is simple. <u>Think of how you'd look if you tried to put your own foot in your mouth. Pretty silly, right? Well, you probably feel the same way when you say something embarrassing.</u>

The expression got its start in the 1700s. Back then, one member of the British Parliament (government), Sir Boyle Roche, was known for saying embarrassing things. He often stumbled over his words and ended up saying things he didn't really mean. One writer described his blunders by saying that every time Roche opened his mouth, he put his foot in it. Presto—a new idiom was born!

# STICK OUT Like a SORE THUMB

Emma came out of her room wearing her favorite pair of jeans. "You're not wearing *those* to the party, are you?" asked her friend Lindsey. "Everyone else is dressing up. You'll stick out like a sore thumb!"

What is Lindsey talking about, and what does she have against thumbs? Ever try holding a pencil or throwing a baseball without one? Yeah, they're kind of important. So what gives?

**This expression refers to something that doesn't seem to belong in its surroundings.** It could be an object—say, a giant truck in a parking lot full of compact cars. Or it might be a person—maybe a senior citizen shopping in a clothing store designed for preteens. If something sticks out like a sore thumb, it's almost impossible to overlook. There's no hiding it—it'll be the first thing almost anybody notices.

If you're wearing something way different from everyone around you, you might feel like you stick out like a sore thumb.

People have been using this idiom for more than four hundred years. It probably refers to a thumb that has been cut and then heavily bandaged. <u>Centuries ago, bandages were thick and heavy. A person with a bandaged thumb wouldn't be able to bend it. It would constantly be sticking out at an odd angle.</u> It would be hard to hide and would be easily noticed by anybody nearby.

# WIN by a NOSE

Thomas could barely contain his excitement. "You should have seen it!" he told his parents. "It was such a close game. It looked bad for a while, but we managed to win by a nose!"

Huh? What sort of game is this? A smelling contest? How else can you use your nose to win something? After all, it just sits there in the middle of your face. It's good for identifying scents and holding up your sunglasses, but not a whole lot more.

**When you've done something by a nose, you've accomplished it by a very slim margin.** Maybe a last-second miracle shot helped you win a basketball game. Or maybe you finished a report for class just minutes before it was due. You've succeeded but just barely.

Noses are mostly good for smelling and holding up sunglasses. How the heck could a nose help you win?

What does a nose have to do with just barely accomplishing something? To find out, we have to turn to horse racing. Imagine two horses charging toward the finish line. They're running neck and neck (hey, another idiom!)—which means very close to each other. They might reach the finish line at almost the same moment. <u>Since a horse's long nose is the first part of its body to cross over the finish line, the winner of a tight race can literally "win by a nose."</u> A similar expression is to "win by a whisker." That's even closer than a nose!

The horse on the inside of the track is ahead of the other by a nose. Will it win? It's hard to say when they're neck and neck!

# TURN the OTHER CHEEK

"What's Jessie's problem?" Tonya asked. "Every time she sees me, she makes fun of me and tries to start a fight."

"Just ignore her," said her brother Mike. "The only thing to do is to turn the other cheek."

What is Mike telling his sister to do? How exactly is one supposed to turn a cheek? And how is that going to help Tonya?

Have you ever had to deal with a snobby kid in school? In this situation, it's sometimes best to turn the other cheek.

This expression is a way of saying that a person should remain peaceful in the face of an attack. If someone calls you a name, you could insult the person right back—or you could turn the other cheek by refusing to return the insult. When you turn the other cheek, you're choosing to keep your anger under control. You're opting not to react in a way you might later regret.

How did turning cheeks become connected to staying peaceful? The expression got started in the Bible. In the New Testament of the Bible, there's a passage that says "Do not resist an evil person. If someone strikes you on the right cheek, turn to him the other also."[1] This means that instead of hitting back if someone hits you on the cheek, you should simply turn your face. That way, you'll be less likely to start a fight.

This guy is turning the other cheek for real. Maybe no one told him that it's just an expression!

# STICK Your NECK OUT

Priya was angry. "Thanks a lot," she said sarcastically to her friend Connor. "I totally stuck my neck out and defended your pitching skills today when Ryan hit a home run off you in phy ed. Then you didn't say anything supportive after I accidentally missed that catch. I just stood there feeling like an idiot."

What does Priya mean she stuck her neck out? How would sticking her neck out help Connor anyway? *Sticking your neck out* **just means you take a risk.** When Priya defended Connor, she might've been teased herself—but she did it anyway to help her friend.

If you defend a friend after he makes a bad move in baseball, then you have stuck your neck out. It's the right thing to do for a buddy.

But why do we say you stick your neck out when you take a risk? It's because the neck is a very vulnerable part of the body. It's right out there for all to see. Yet it's also really important. After all, it holds up your entire head. Just think where you'd be without it!

This expression probably comes from the way that butchers kill chickens for food. A butcher pulls a chicken's neck out so that it can be chopped off. As you can imagine, this isn't a good situation for the chicken. Similarly, Priya put herself in a potentially risky spot when she defended Connor. But fortunately, Priya wasn't in any danger of having her neck chopped off. In fact, compared to chickens, Priya has it pretty easy!

A butcher's method for preparing chicken may have inspired the phrase stick your neck out.

# PULLING Your LEG

Rose could barely keep a straight face while she talked to her grandma on the phone. "We won the lottery, Grandma!" she said. "We're going to be millionaires!"

Rose's grandma gasped with surprise. "What? Oh, my! You won the lottery?" she asked. Rose couldn't help but laugh then. "No, not really, Grandma. I was just pulling your leg."

Say what? What's this about pulling on legs? Legs are for walking on, not pulling!

**Of course, Rose wasn't actually pulling anybody's leg. She was just using an expression that means she was playing a joke.** She was letting her grandma know she was only kidding.

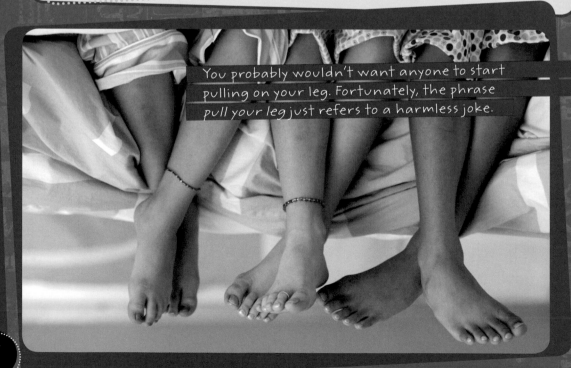

You probably wouldn't want anyone to start pulling on your leg. Fortunately, the phrase *pull your leg* just refers to a harmless joke.

But why does saying you're pulling someone's leg mean you're kidding him or her? This one's a little tricky. <u>Some say that years ago, thieves would reach out and grab a victim's leg to trip him or her before stealing the person's money.</u> Over time, the phrase *pulling your leg* came to mean that the joke was on you. Another explanation says that when criminals were hanged in public, onlookers would come up to them and pull on their legs. Again, the "joke" was on the people whose legs were being pulled.

Whichever theory is correct, you don't have to worry about being robbed—or even worse, hanged—when you hear the phrase *pulling your leg*. It just means that somebody's playing a joke on you.

# TAKE IT on the CHIN

Tony walked out of class one day with a frown on his face.

"What's wrong?" asked Eva.

"I forgot to study for the social studies test," he admitted. "I really took it on the chin today."

Have you ever tried to take a test while it was on your chin? How would that even work? Obviously, something else is going on here. Just what did Tony take, and what was it doing on his chin?

**When you take it on the chin, you're suffering a defeat or a setback of some sort.** A football team might take it on the chin if they lose a big game. Or an actress might take it on the chin if she forgets her lines in the middle of a play.

What on earth does it mean to take it on the chin? It means that you've suffered a setback. Maybe that's why this kid looks glum.

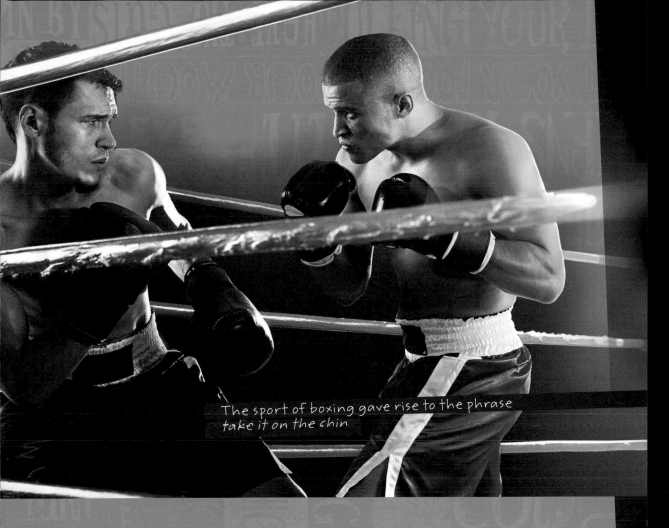

The sport of boxing gave rise to the phrase *take it on the chin*

But where does this expression come from? The answer lies in the sport of boxing. <u>The chin is one of the most vulnerable spots for a boxer. A punch to the face or the body might hurt, but a punch just below the chin can be the most devastating of all.</u> It snaps the head back violently. This motion often sends the boxer to the mat, out cold. One thing is true for both boxing and life. When you take one on the chin, all you can do is brush yourself off and get back up again.

# A CHIP on Your SHOULDER

"Every time I try to talk to Grant, he's mean to me," Hanna told her friend Amir. "What's his problem? Why does he have such a chip on his shoulder?"

Hmm. What's Hanna talking about here? Potato chips? Poker chips? And why does having a chip on his shoulder make Grant so grouchy?

Grant doesn't actually have a chip on his shoulder. This is just a way of saying that Grant seems mad or upset about something. He seems like he wants to argue or pick a fight.

Look out for this guy. He's got a real chip on his shoulder.

The idiom comes to us from docks of the British Royal Navy in the 1700s. Dockworkers were allowed to take small cuts of lumber called chips home with them. They could use the lumber for their own personal projects. They carried the lumber out on their shoulders. But in 1756, the navy changed its policy. Dockworkers could only take home chips that they carried under their arms—a far smaller amount. This rule change was unpopular with the dockworkers. They sometimes tried to take home larger amounts.

No, the phrase chip on your shoulder has nothing to do with these kinds of chips!

Anyone who tried to carry out a large chip over his shoulder was just waiting for someone to challenge him.

In the 1800s, some U.S. men took this idiom literally. They would put a small chip of wood on their shoulders, daring someone to knock it off. The chip was really just an invitation for a fight.

# GIVING the COLD SHOULDER

"I just don't know what to do about Keisha," Ted told his friends at lunch. "We had an argument yesterday, and she's been giving me the cold shoulder ever since."

What's this about? What does an argument have to do with Keisha's shoulder being cold? Why not a hot ankle or a lukewarm elbow? And if her shoulder is really so cold, why doesn't she just grab a nice warm sweater?

You've probably figured out that Keisha's shoulder isn't really cold. **If someone is giving you the cold shoulder, then that person is ignoring you or trying to make you feel unwelcome.** Maybe he or she is rude or won't talk to you. Or perhaps the person gives only cool, short answers to your questions.

Yikes—this girl is totally giving her friend the cold shoulder!

So where does this expression come from? Not everyone
agrees. Some people think it started hundreds of years ago. <u>Back
then, people welcomed most visitors to their homes with a
hot meal. But unwelcome visitors got only a cold shoulder
of mutton (sheep meat).</u> Others say that the expression has
nothing to do with mutton. They believe that the writer Sir Walter
Scott invented the phrase in the 1800s. It referred to one person
turning away from another—or rudely showing a shoulder instead
of the face. In either case, getting a cold shoulder isn't much fun.

# COSTS an ARM and a LEG

Hank's parents let him have a cell phone under one condition. He had to pay for any calls or texts that went over the limit that his plan allowed. Hank groaned as he reviewed this month's bill with his dad. "I'm fifty texts over the limit?" he asked. "That'll cost me five dollars. That's half my allowance! Why can't I have a plan that doesn't cost me an arm and a leg?"

A pricey cell phone bill is bad enough. But having to give up body parts? That sounds just terrible! Why would anyone have to lose their limbs for a cell phone plan?

If something costs you big bucks, you might say you paid an arm and a leg.

It's no time to panic. Hank's phone provider only wants his money, not his body parts. **This expression is merely a way of saying that something is really expensive.** Maybe it's the texting fees on your cell phone. Or maybe it's that new video game that you just *have* to have. Either way, the pain you feel comes from all the zeroes on the bill or price tag, not from anyone hacking off an arm or a leg.

This expression became popular around the 1950s. Most people think it came from the idiom "I'd give my right arm" for something, which is a way of saying you'd pay a hefty price for it. A popular story says it grew out of an old practice in which painters charged customers for portraits based on how many limbs they painted. But this isn't true. Painters often charged by the size of the portrait—but they never charged people based on how many limbs they had to paint. If they had, then getting your portrait painted might've been an even worse deal than having to pay for lots of calls and texts!

# TURN a BLIND EYE

Dani felt upset after her teacher told her class that there are lots of hungry kids around the world. "So many kids in our country don't even pay attention to what's going on in other places," she told her friend Mackenzie. "It sometimes feels like we turn a blind eye to some really important problems."

Finding out about hungry kids is a good reason to feel upset. But what does Dani mean when she says people turn a blind eye? After all, a blind eye couldn't see anything no matter where you pointed it, right?

**This expression is a way of saying that a person is choosing to ignore something unpleasant or unpopular.** You might turn a blind eye to another student being bullied. Or you could turn a blind eye to someone cheating on a test. Instead of really looking at the problem, you choose to pretend it doesn't exist.

Sometimes it can seem like we close our eyes and ears to some really big problems. When that happens, you might say we're turning a blind eye.

<u>We have Admiral Horatio Nelson to thank for this idiom.</u>
Centuries ago, Nelson was an officer in the British Royal Navy. A wound left him blind in one eye. In 1801, Nelson was in command of the British fleet at the Battle of Copenhagen in Copenhagen, Denmark. The Royal Navy used a system of signal flags to communicate. At one point, Nelson's superiors (those in charge of him) ordered him to withdraw. But Nelson disagreed with the order. He didn't want to withdraw. So he raised a small telescope to his blind eye and pointed it toward the flags. Then he announced, "I have only one eye, and I have a right to be blind sometimes. I really do not see the signal." He ignored the order, and an idiom was born.

We have Horatio Nelson to thank for the phrase *turn a blind eye.*

# An EYE for an EYE

A.J. sat slumped over in the principal's office. "So why did you do it, young man? What made you tear up your classmate's social studies report?" asked Principal Hernandez.

A.J. shrugged. "He spilled soda all over mine and ruined it. It was an eye for an eye."

Yikes—that sounds intense. A report is important, but not nearly as important as an eye. Wouldn't everything be better if we all just left one another's eyes alone?

If this idiom sounds like serious business, that's because it is. **An eye for an eye is a way of saying that whatever one person does to another, he or she should get back in turn.** It may be simple payback for a minor wrong. Or it may be giving the death penalty to someone found guilty of murder.

This kid took an eye for an eye—but now he's in big trouble.

This expression goes way back to a time when people followed an idea called the law of retribution. It appeared in the Old Testament of the Bible as well as in the Code of Hammurabi. Hammurabi was the king of ancient Babylon (part of modern-day Iraq) almost four thousand years ago. His laws said that, literally, if one person destroyed another person's eye, then that person should have his or her eye destroyed in return. Grim but true! Maybe it's not so bad living in the twenty-first century, huh?

Here's a stone carving of Hammurabi, who started the idea of taking an eye for an eye.

# Glossary

**blunder:** a mistake

**fleet:** a number of warships under a single command

**idiom:** a commonly used expression or phrase that means something different from what it appears to mean

**margin:** a small amount

**mutton:** meat from a sheep

**Parliament:** the group that makes laws in the United Kingdom

**portrait:** a painting or other image of a person

**retribution:** the act of punishing someone for something bad that he or she did

**superior:** a boss, or someone who is in charge of someone else

**withdraw:** to pull back military forces from an attack

# Source Notes

13  Bible Study Tools, 2012. http://www.biblestudytools.com/matthew/5-39-compare.html (May 17, 2012).

27  David Tudor Davies, *Nelson's Navy: English Fighting Ships, 1793–1815* (Mechanicsburg, PA: Stackpole Books, 1996), 126.

# Further Reading

Amoroso, Cynthia. *I'm All Thumbs!: (And Other Odd Things We Say)*. Mankato, MN: Child's World, 2011. Learn more about some of the English language's strangest idioms and why we say the things we say.

Atkinson, Mary. *What Do You Mean?: Communication Isn't Easy*. New York: Children's Press, 2007. Learn about all sorts of things that can confuse communication, from idioms to changing word meanings to slang and different pronunciations.

Doeden, Matt. *Get Your Nose Out of Joint: And Other Medical Expressions*. Minneapolis: Lerner Publications Company, 2013. Discover the meaning and history behind thirteen common expressions related to medicine and health.

The Idiom Connection
http://www.idiomconnection.com
The Idiom Connection has tons of easy-to-search explanations of the most common English idioms. Search alphabetically or by theme.

Idiom Site
http://www.idiomsite.com
Check out this website for an alphabetical list of expressions and what they mean.

Moses, Will. *Raining Cats and Dogs*. New York: Philomel Books, 2008. This book offers a humorous approach to investigating idioms and what they really mean.

Paint by Idioms
http://www.funbrain.com/funbrain/idioms
Check out this simple game. Answer questions about common idioms and watch as a funny picture is painted with every correct answer.

Terban, Marvin. *In a Pickle: And Other Funny Idioms*. New York: Clarion Books, 2007. Through lively text and illustrations, Terban investigates thirty strange expressions, including *in a pickle* and *don't cry over spilled milk*.

Walton, Rick. *Why the Banana Split: An Adventure in Idioms*. Salt Lake City: Gibbs Smith, 2011. In this fictional story, Walton pokes fun at strange expressions as he tells the tale of a town threatened by a fruit-eating *Tyrannosaurus rex*.

# Index

# Photo Acknowledgments

The images in this book are used with the permission of: © iStockphoto.com/Alija, p. 5; © Kwame Zikomo/SuperStock, p. 6; © David Sutherland/Photographer's Choice/ Getty Images, p. 8; © Arthur Tilley/Photodisc/Getty Images, p. 10; © Patrick Donehue/ Stone/Getty Images, p. 11; © iStockphoto.com/Dawn Lackner, p. 12; © Ian Murray/ Photographer's Choice/Getty Images, p. 13; © iStockphoto.com/james boulette, p. 14; © iStockphoto.com/Lauri Patterson, p. 15; © Jeremy Samuelson/Taxi/Getty Images, p. 16; © disiming/Alamy, p. 18; © Image Source/Getty Images, p. 19; © Digital Vision/ Getty Images, p. 20; © iStockphoto.com/NoDerog, p. 21; © iStockphoto.com/Tari Faris, p. 22; © mmaxer/Shutterstock.com, p. 25; © Design Pics/Con Tanasiuk/Getty Images, p. 26; © Hulton Archive/Getty Images, p. 27; © Katrina Wittkamp/Digital Vision/Getty Images, p. 28; © INTERFOTO/Alamy, p. 29.

Front cover artwork: © Tim Parlin/Independent Picture Service.
Front cover photography: © Giliane Mansfeldt/Independent Picture Service.

Main body text set in Adrianna Light 11/17.
Typeface provided by Chank.